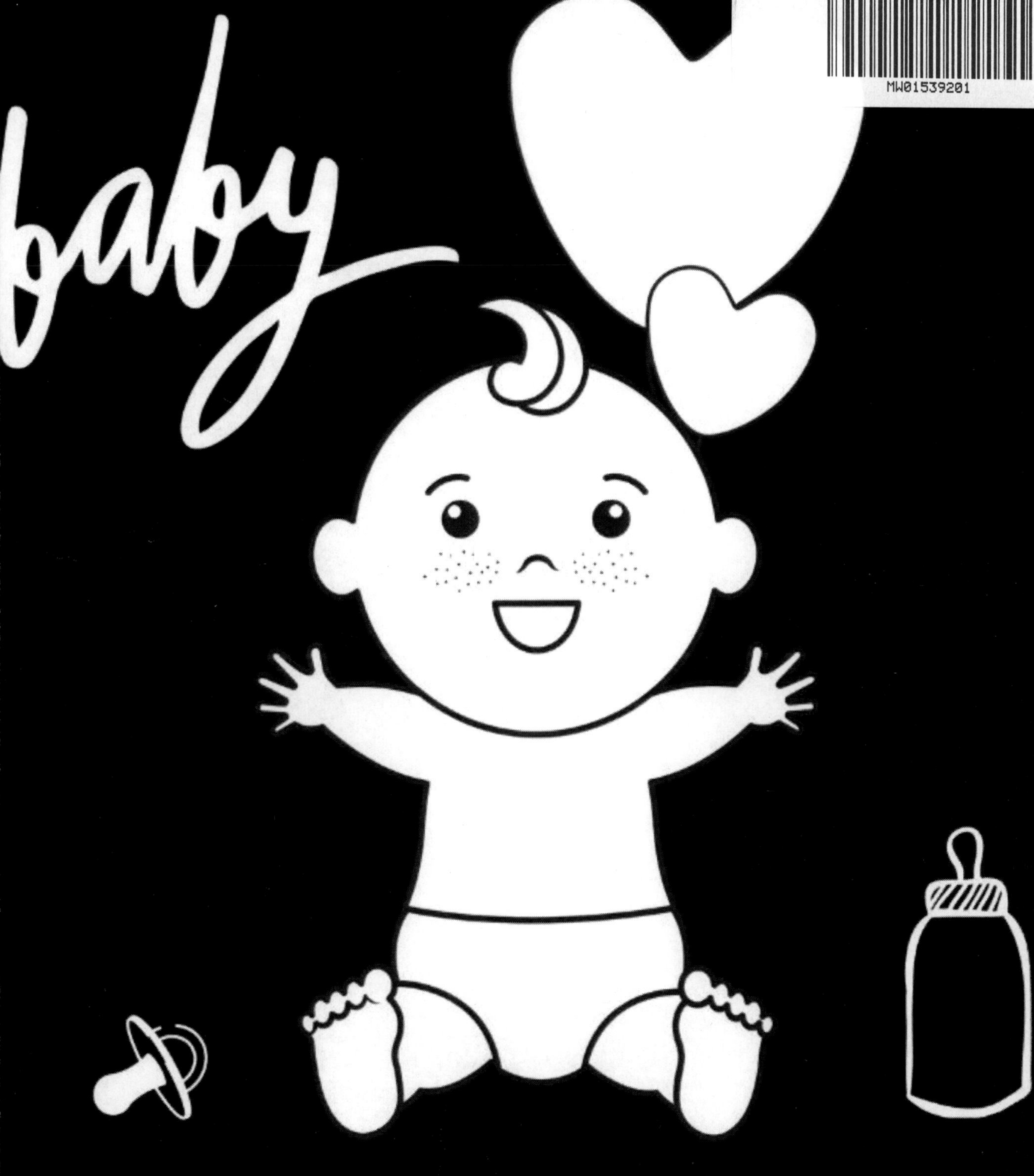
baby

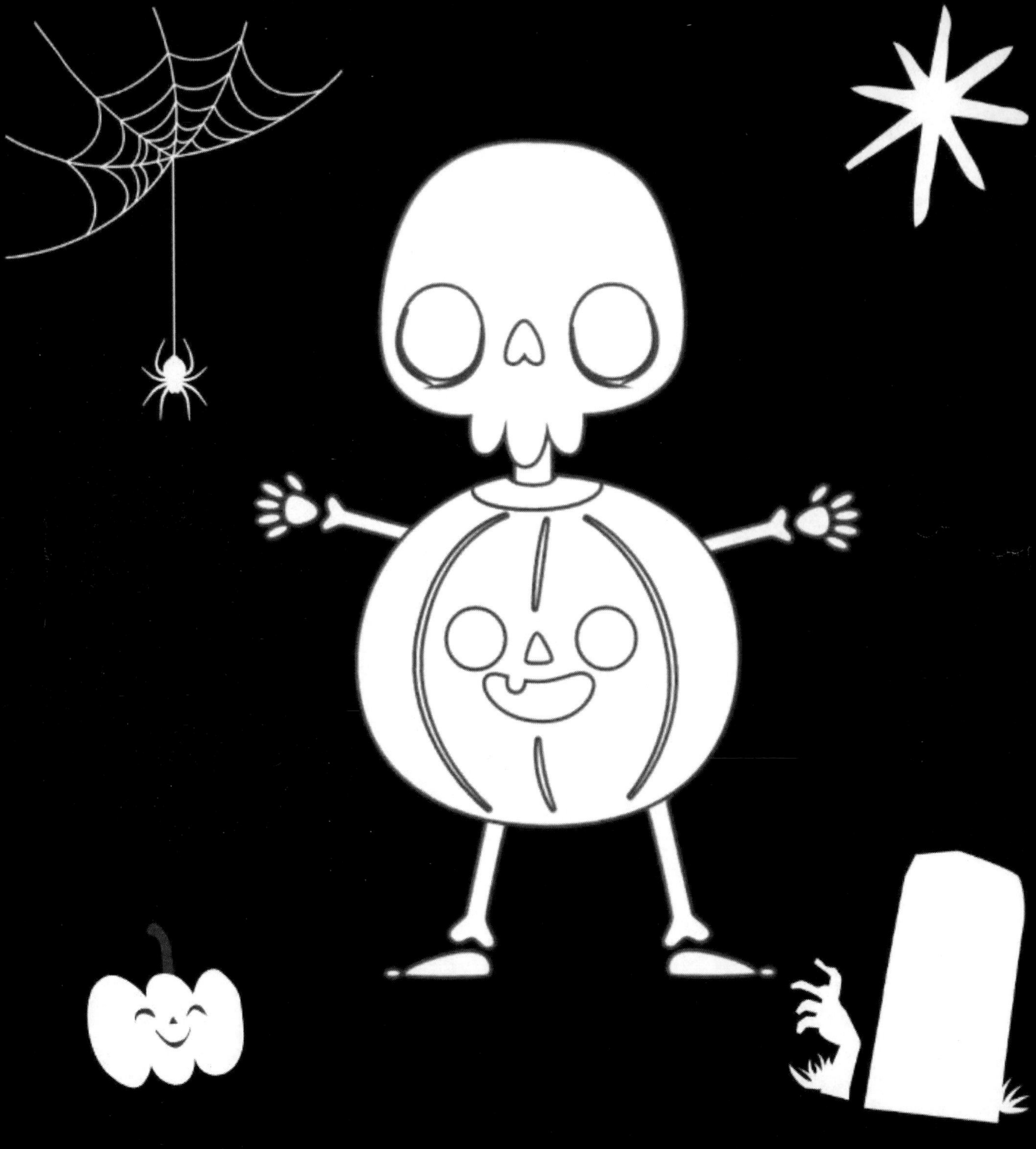

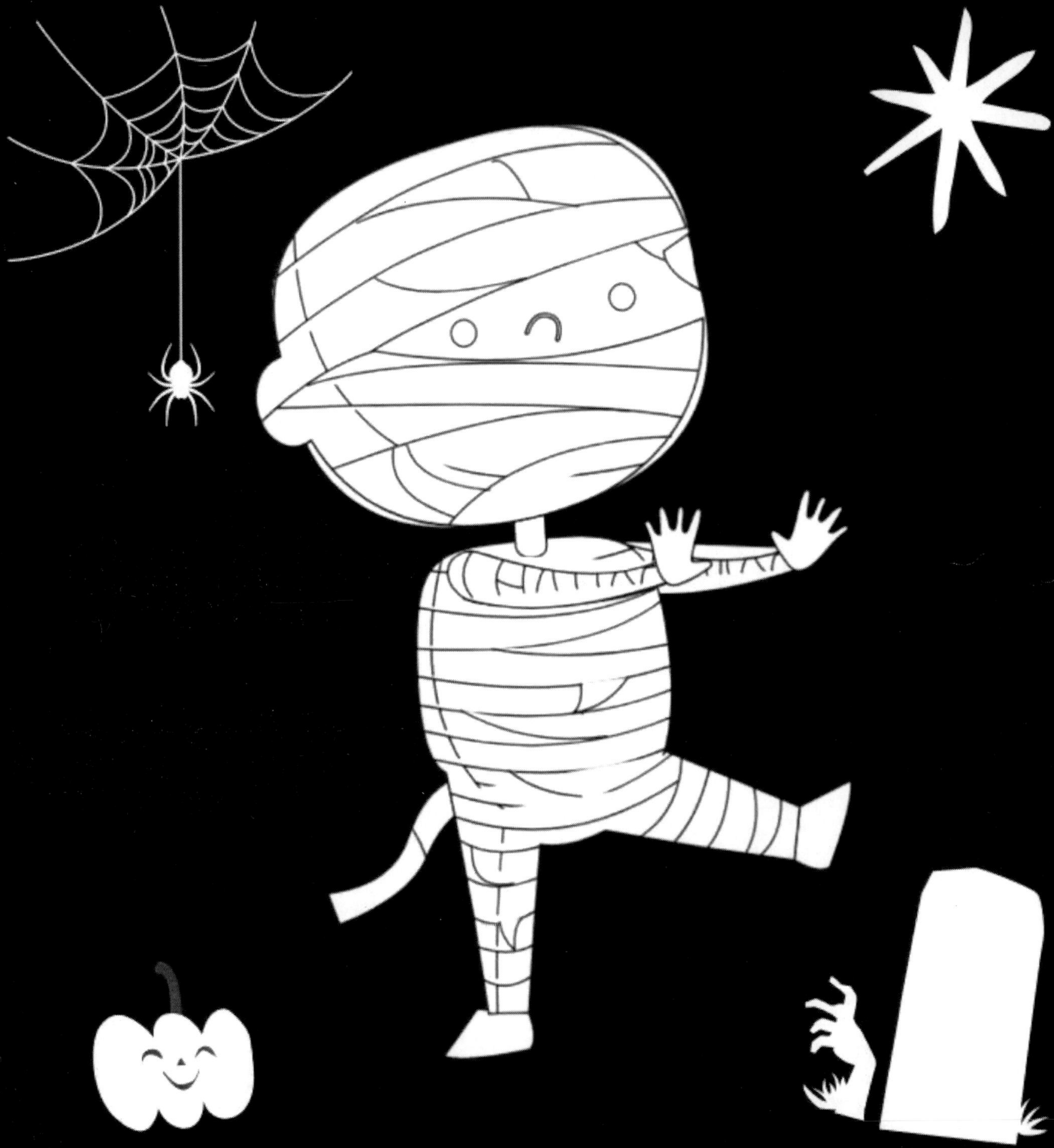

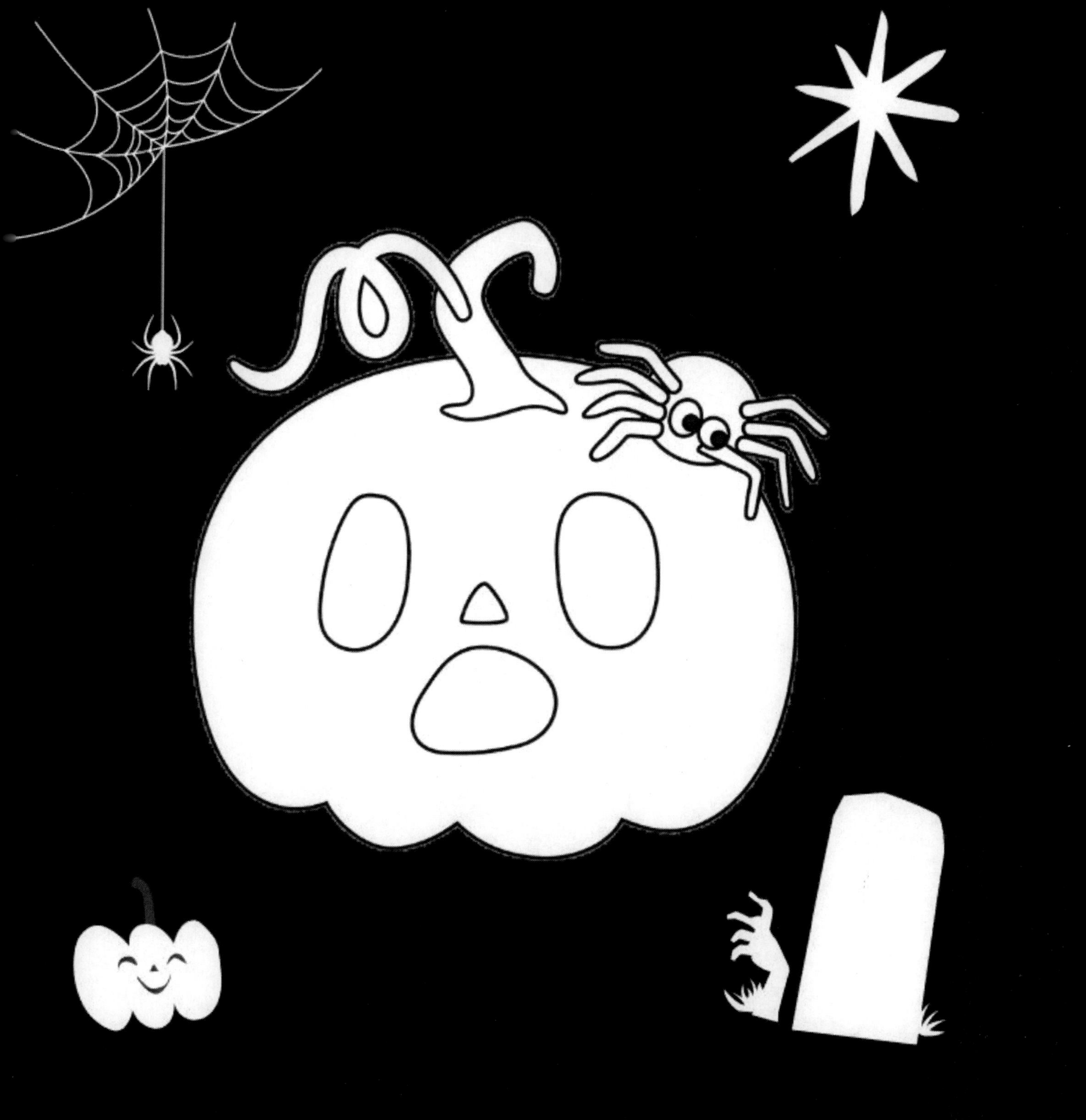

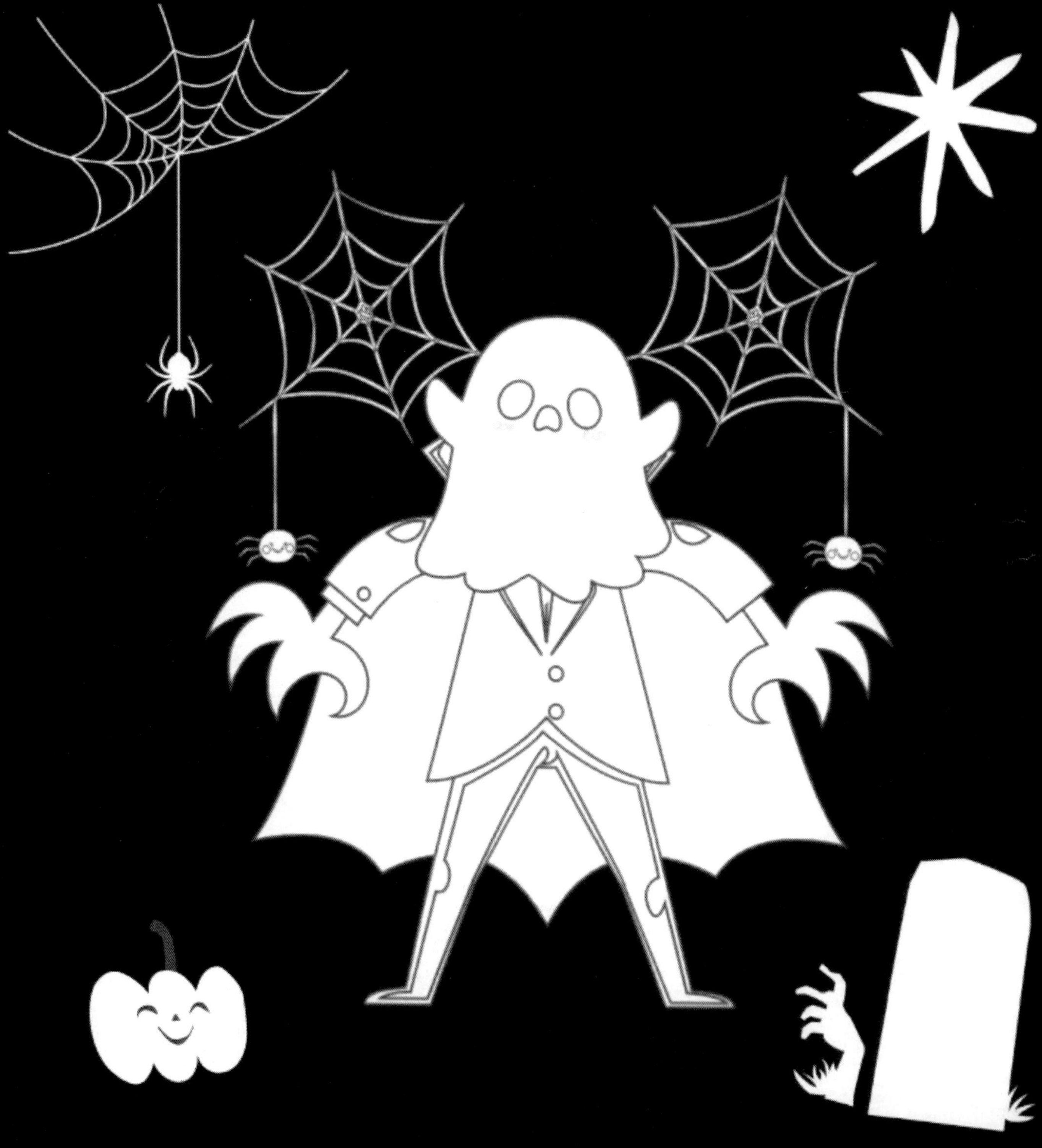

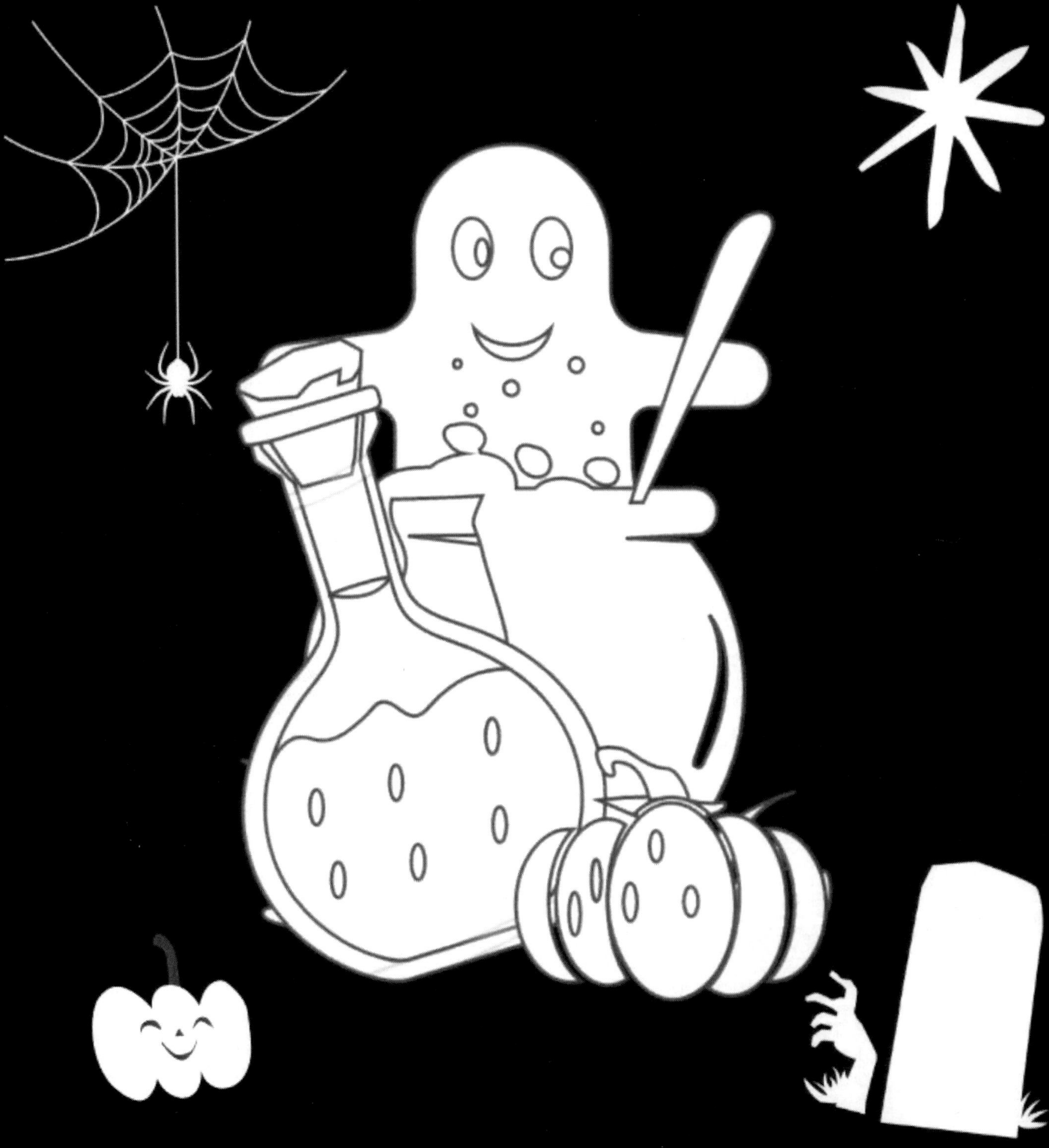

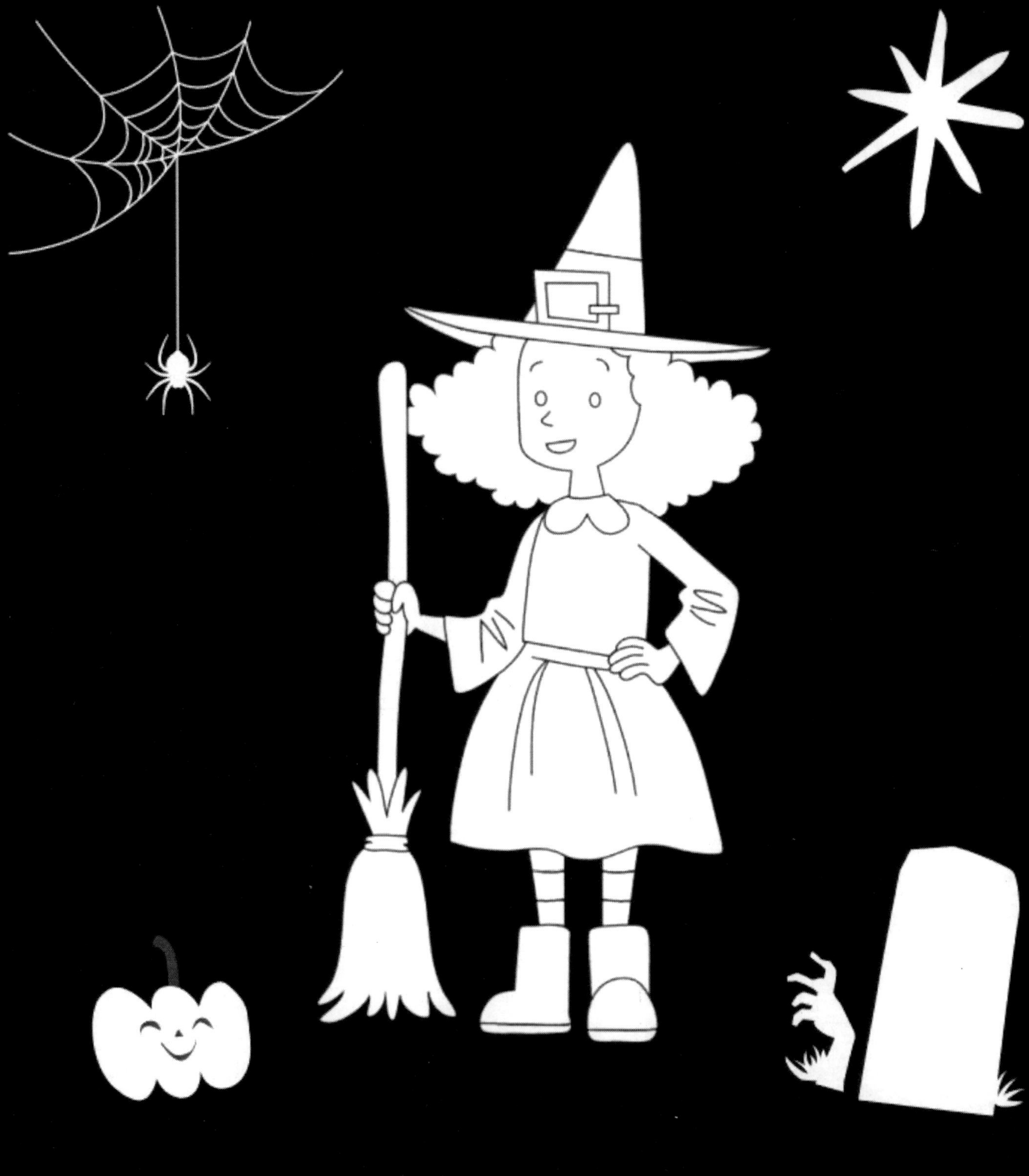

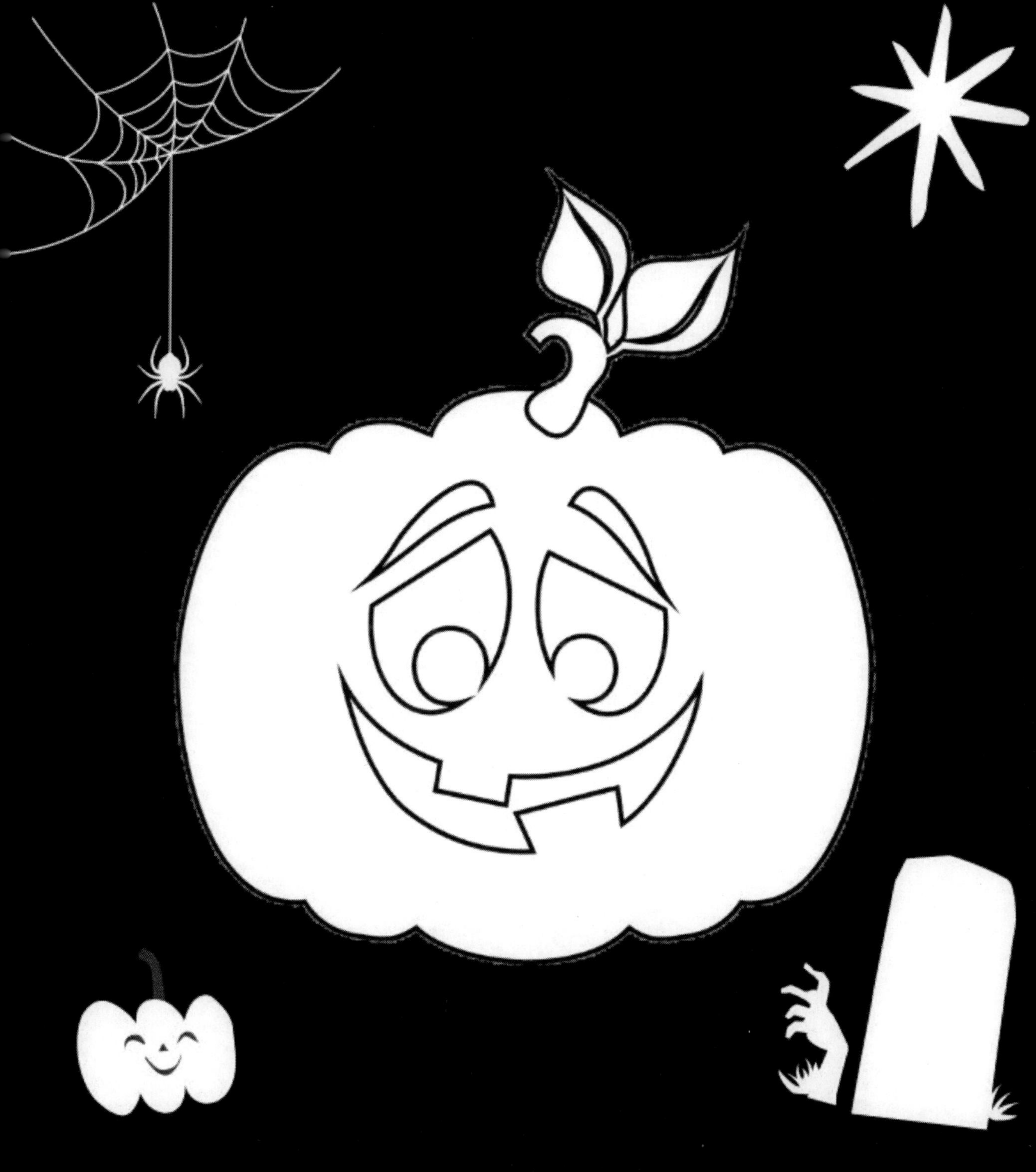

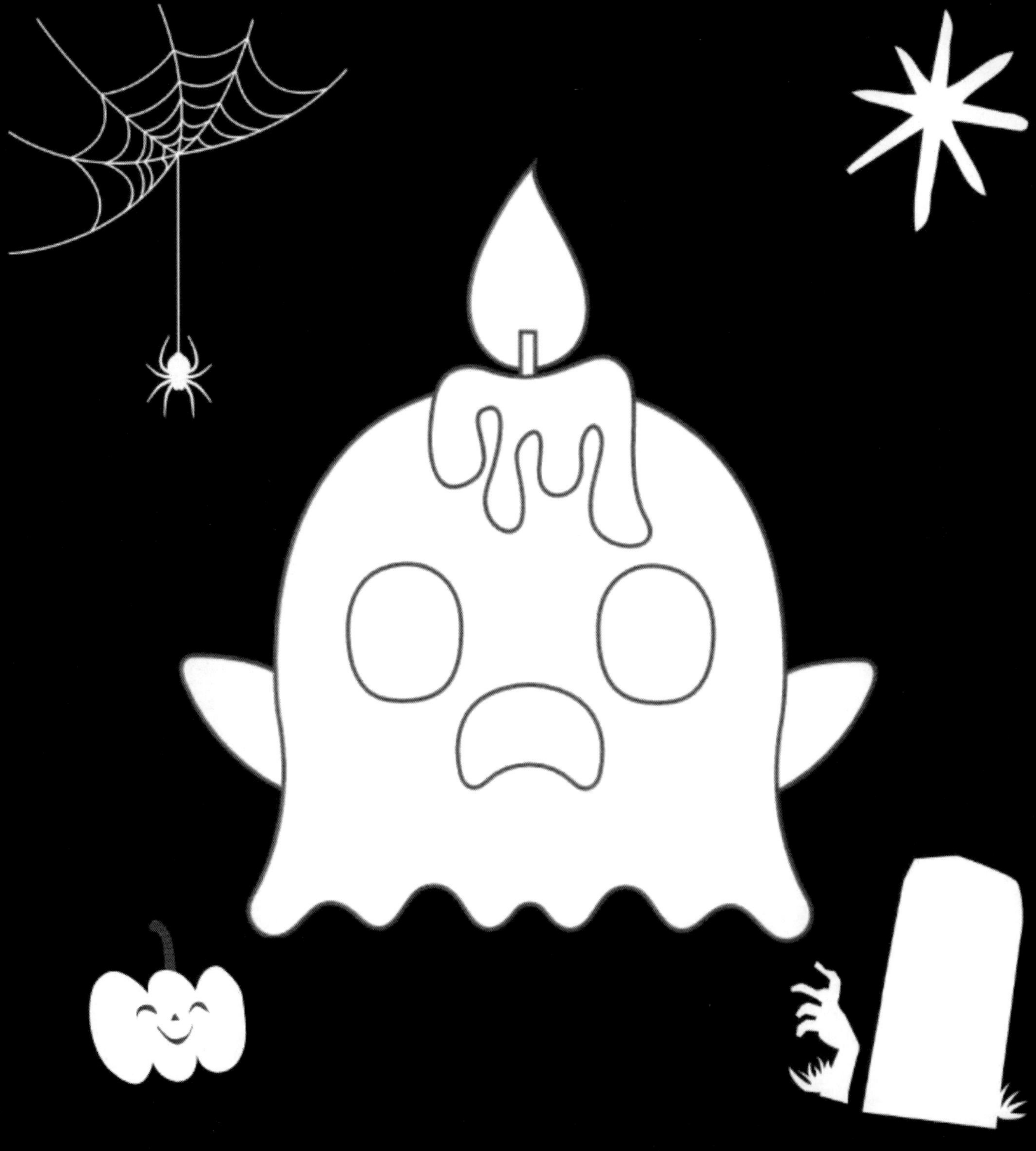

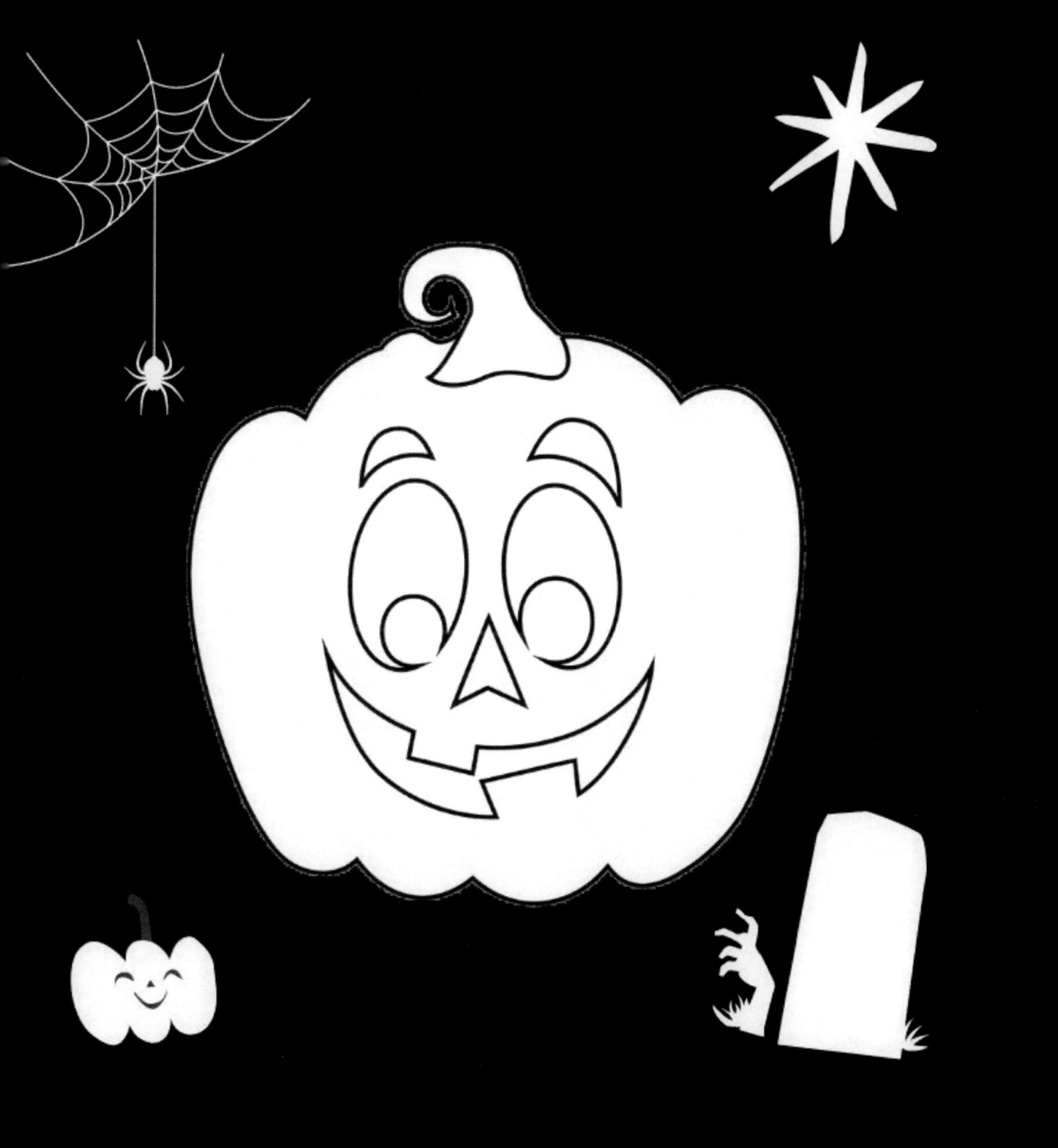

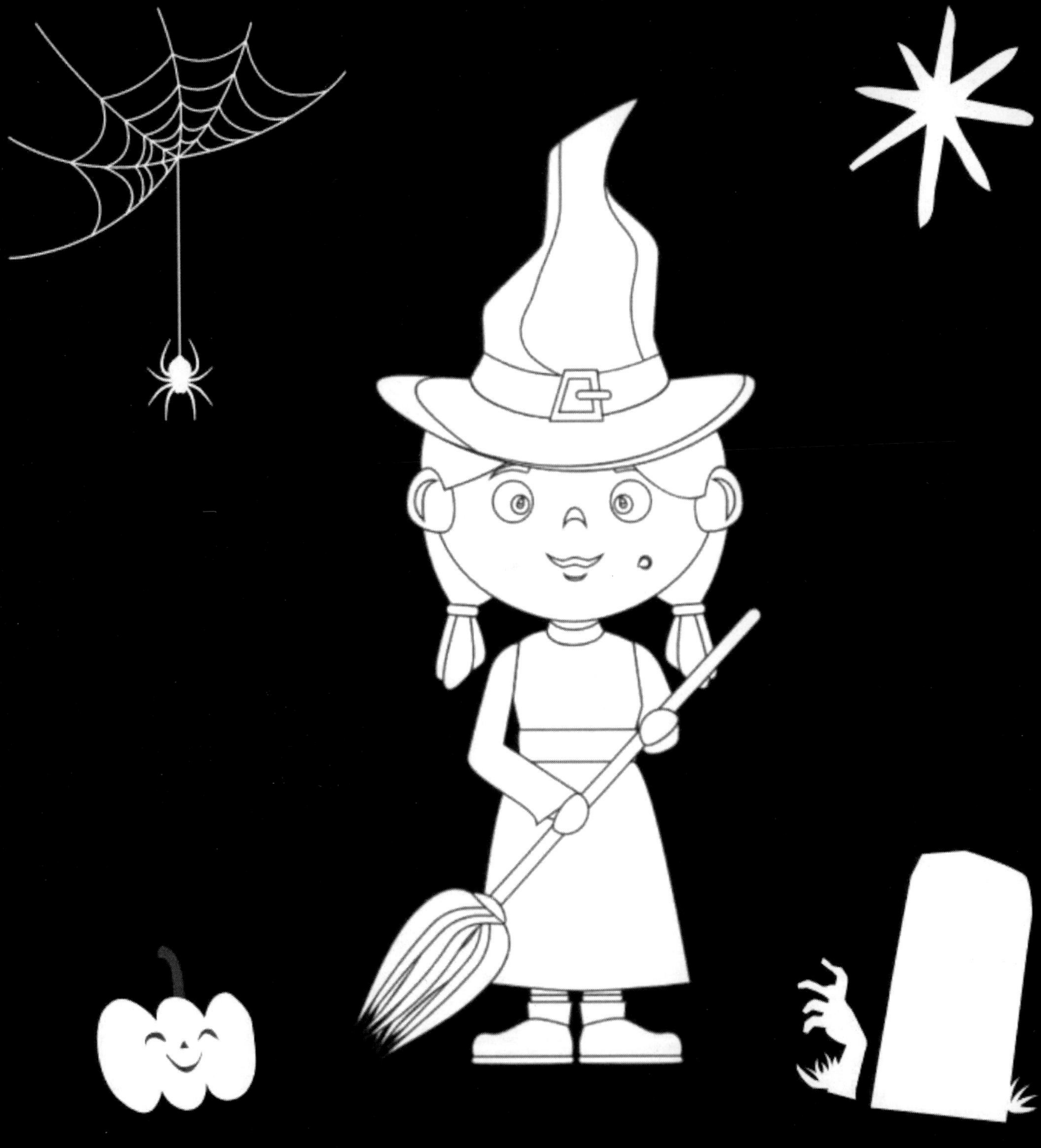

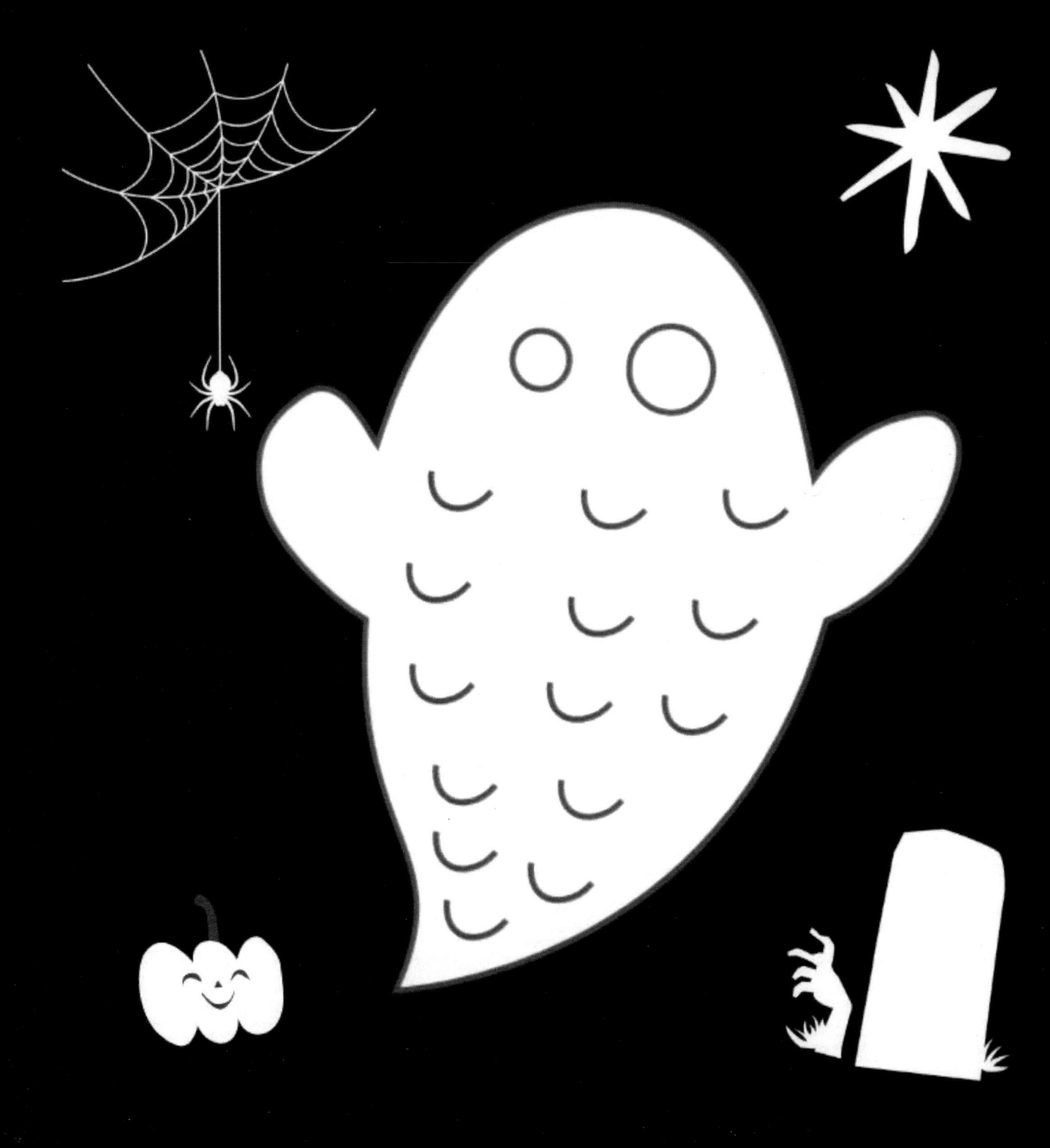

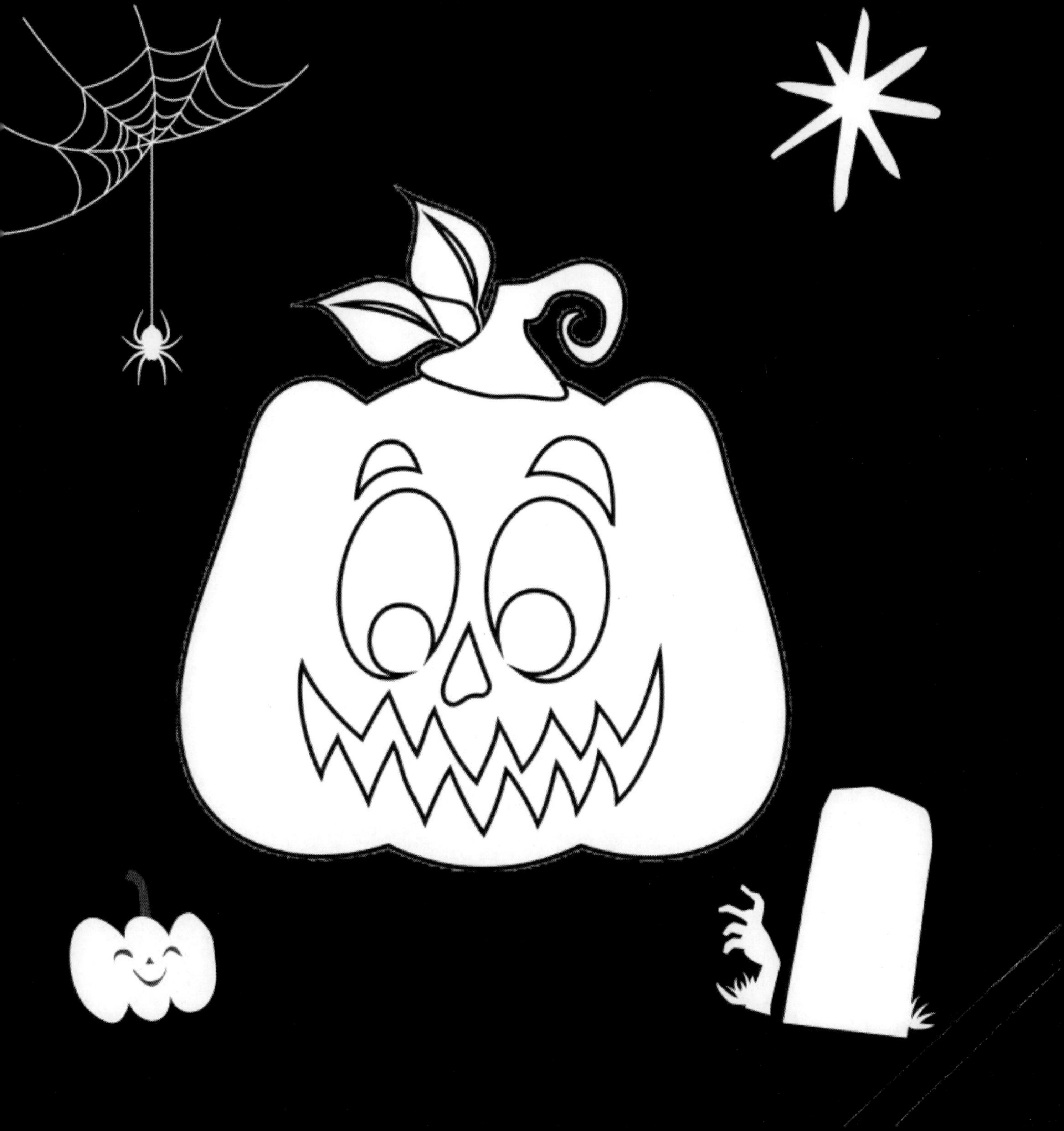

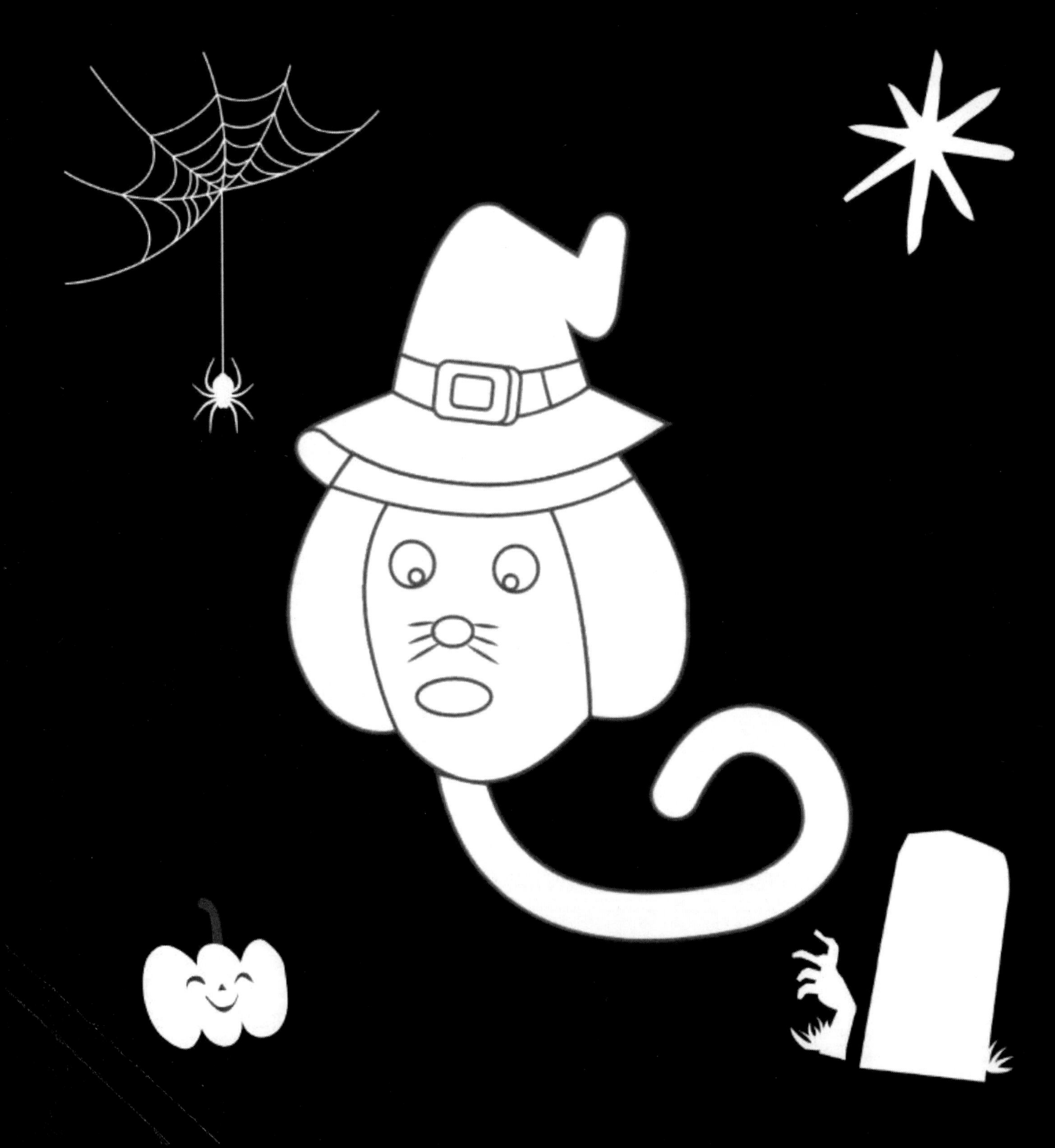

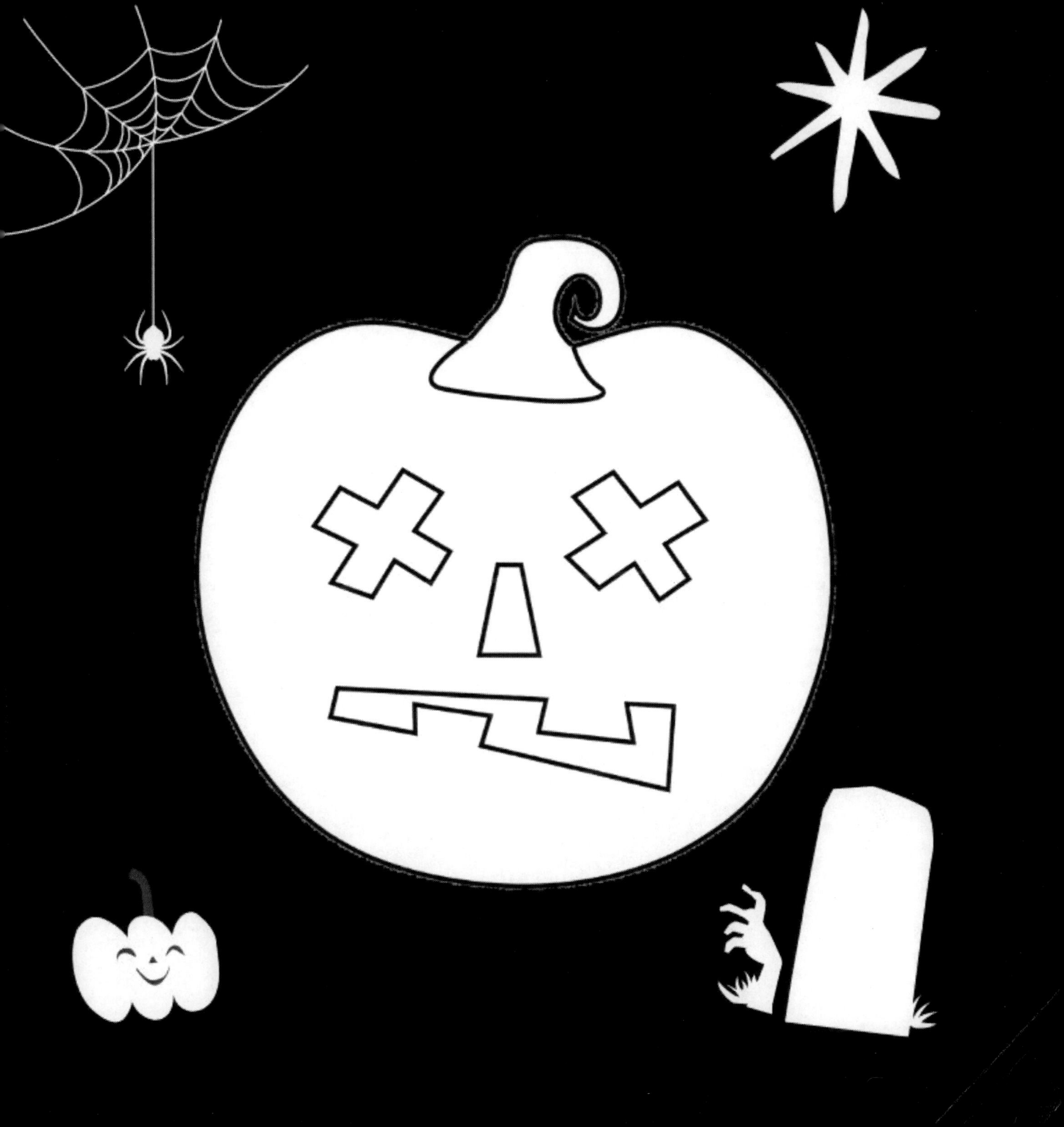

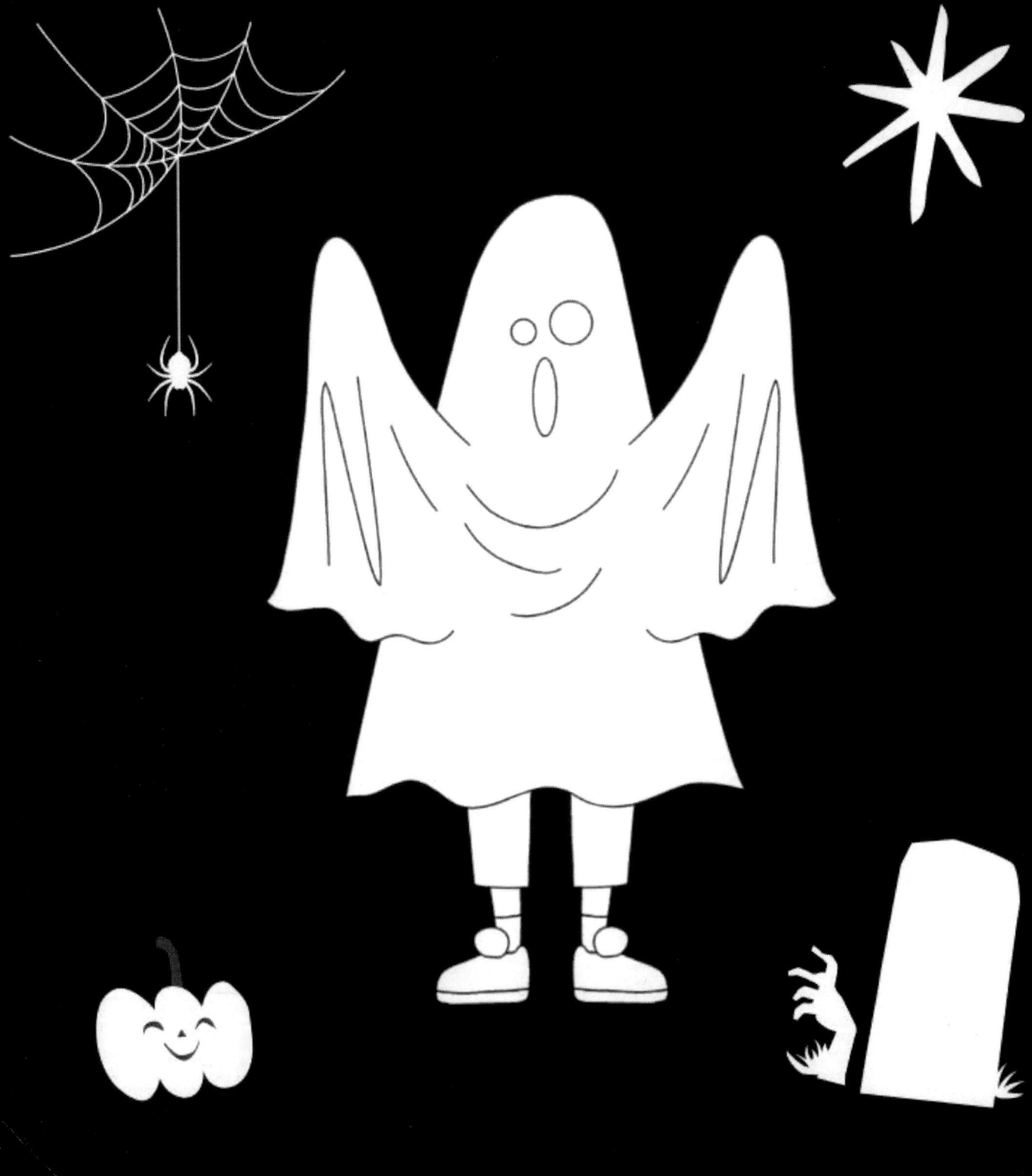

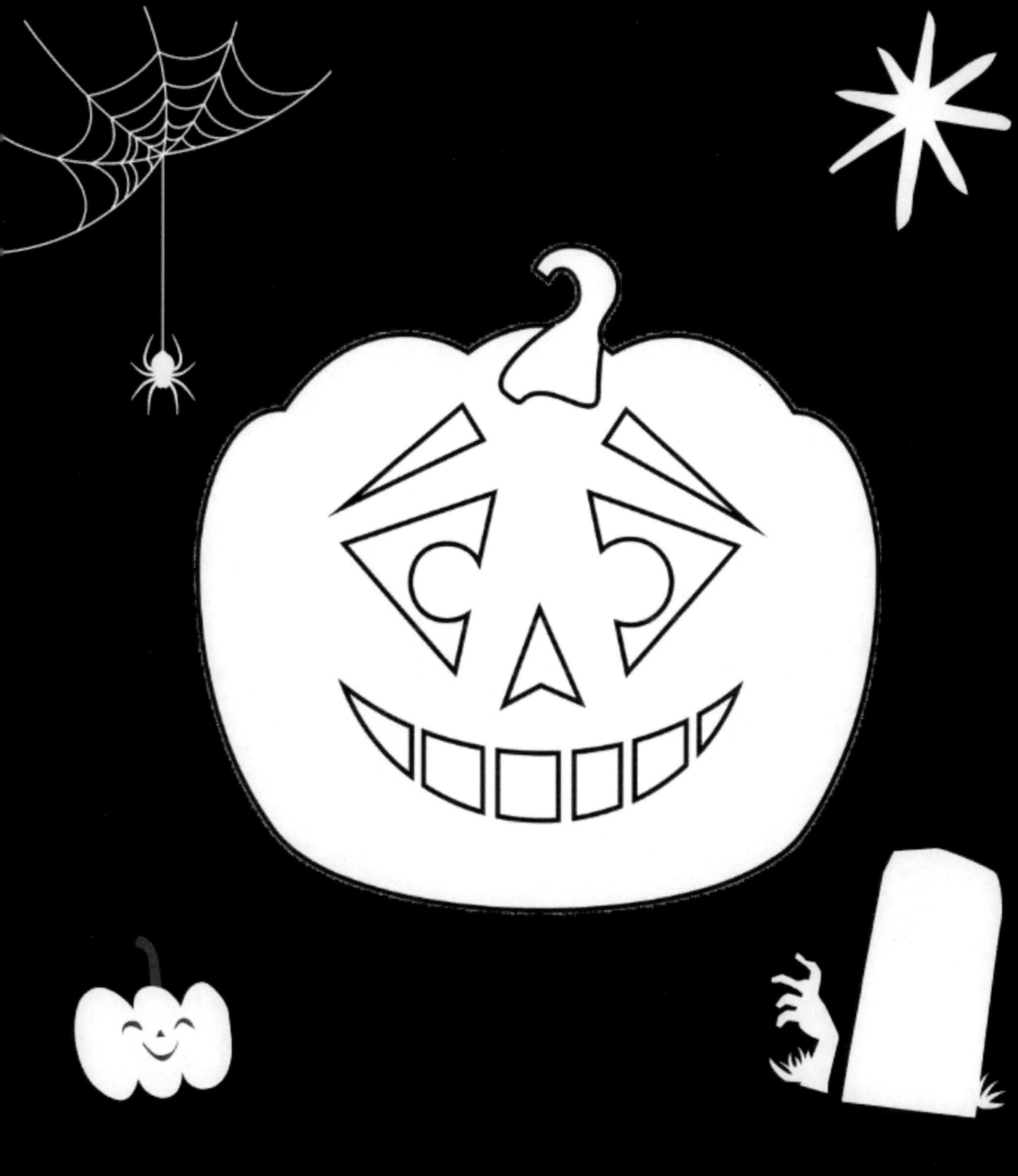

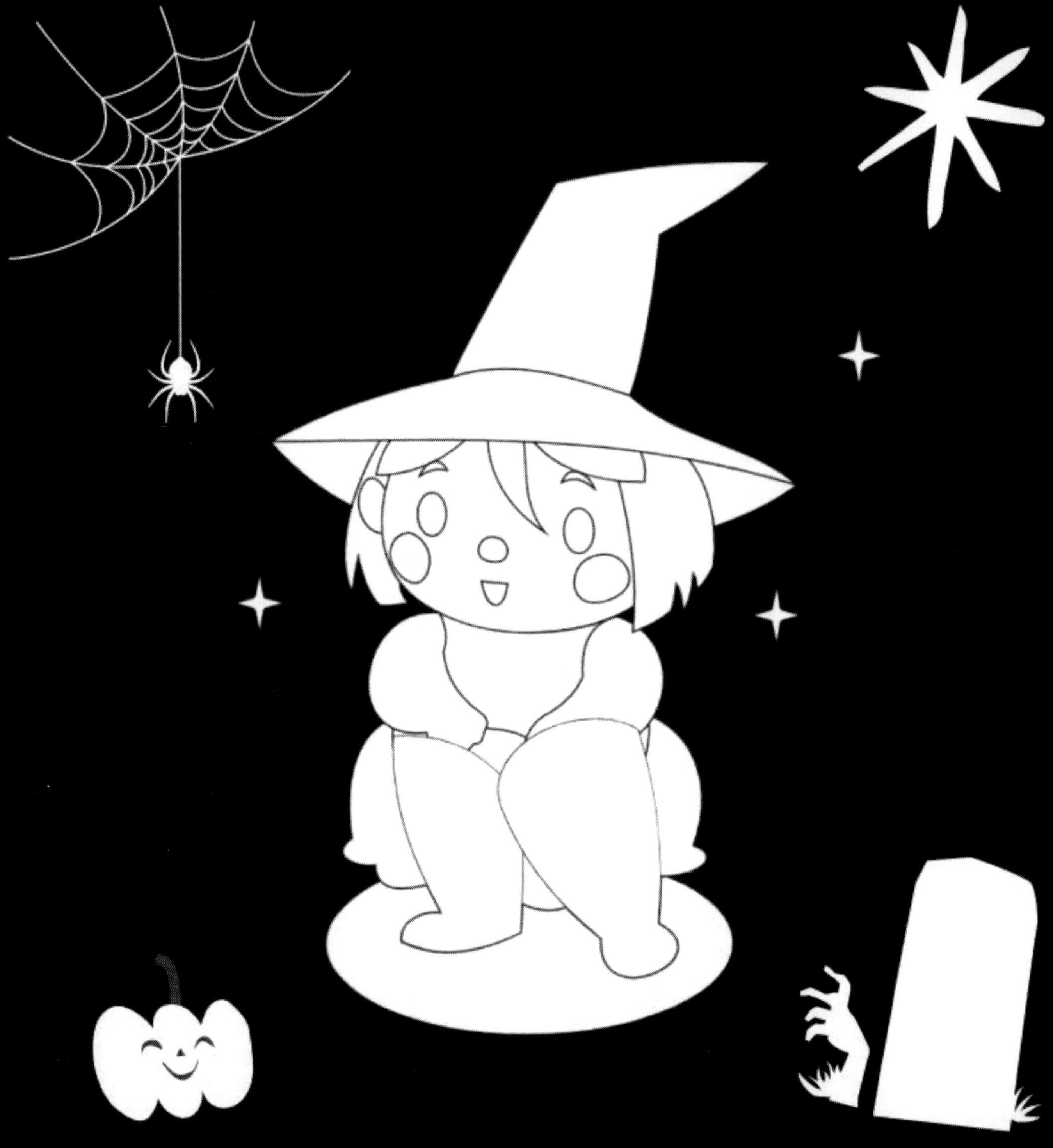

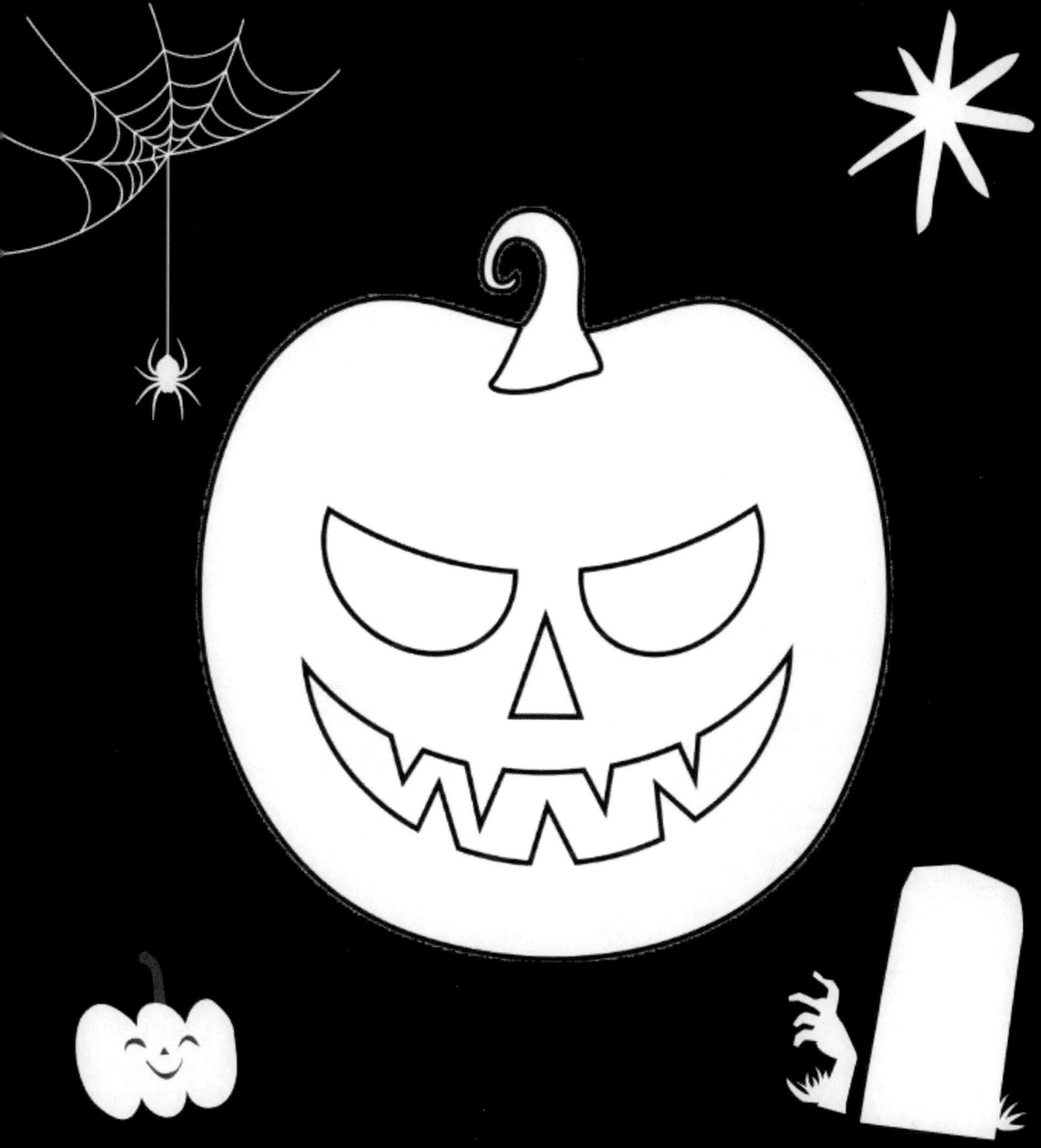

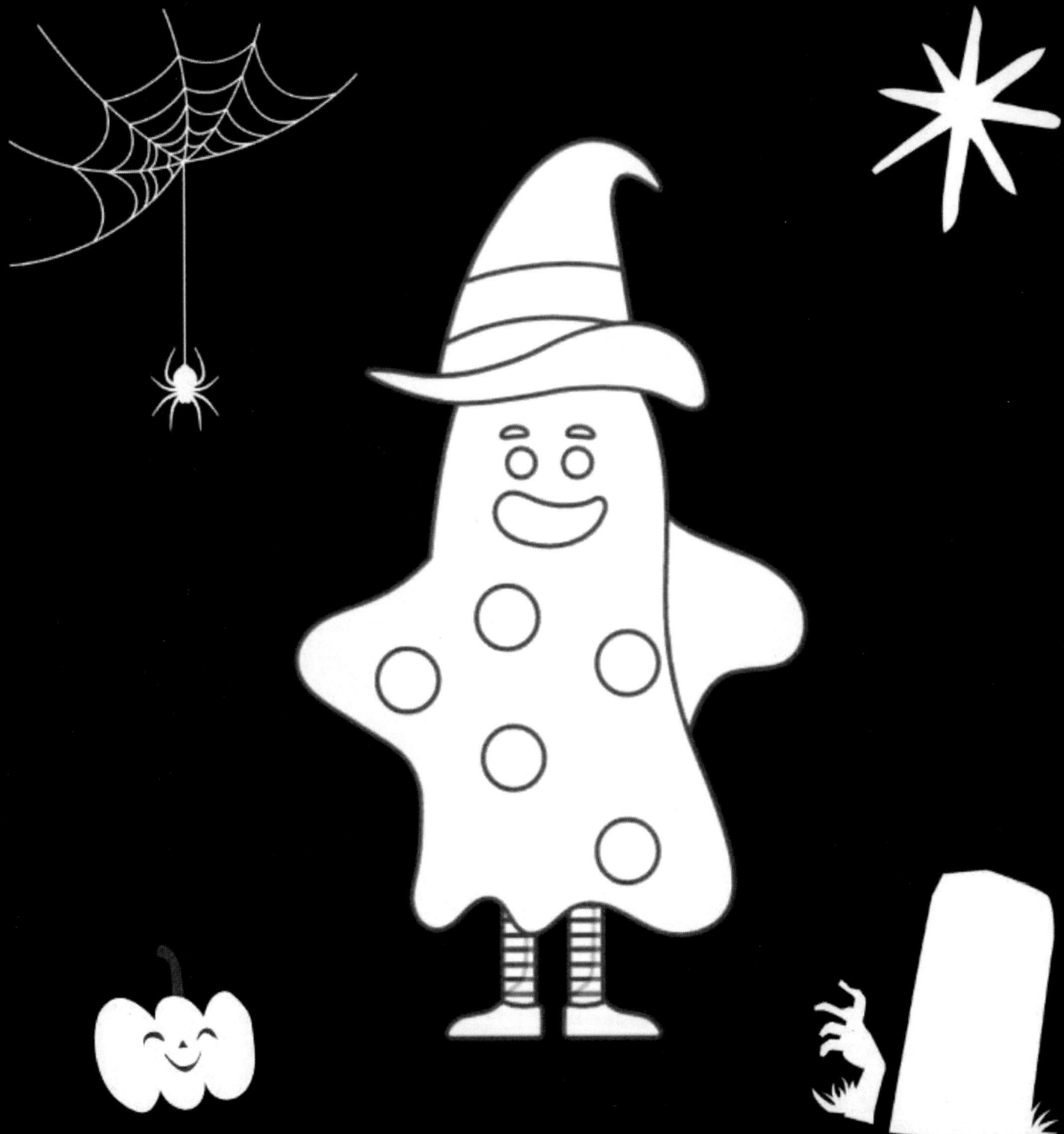

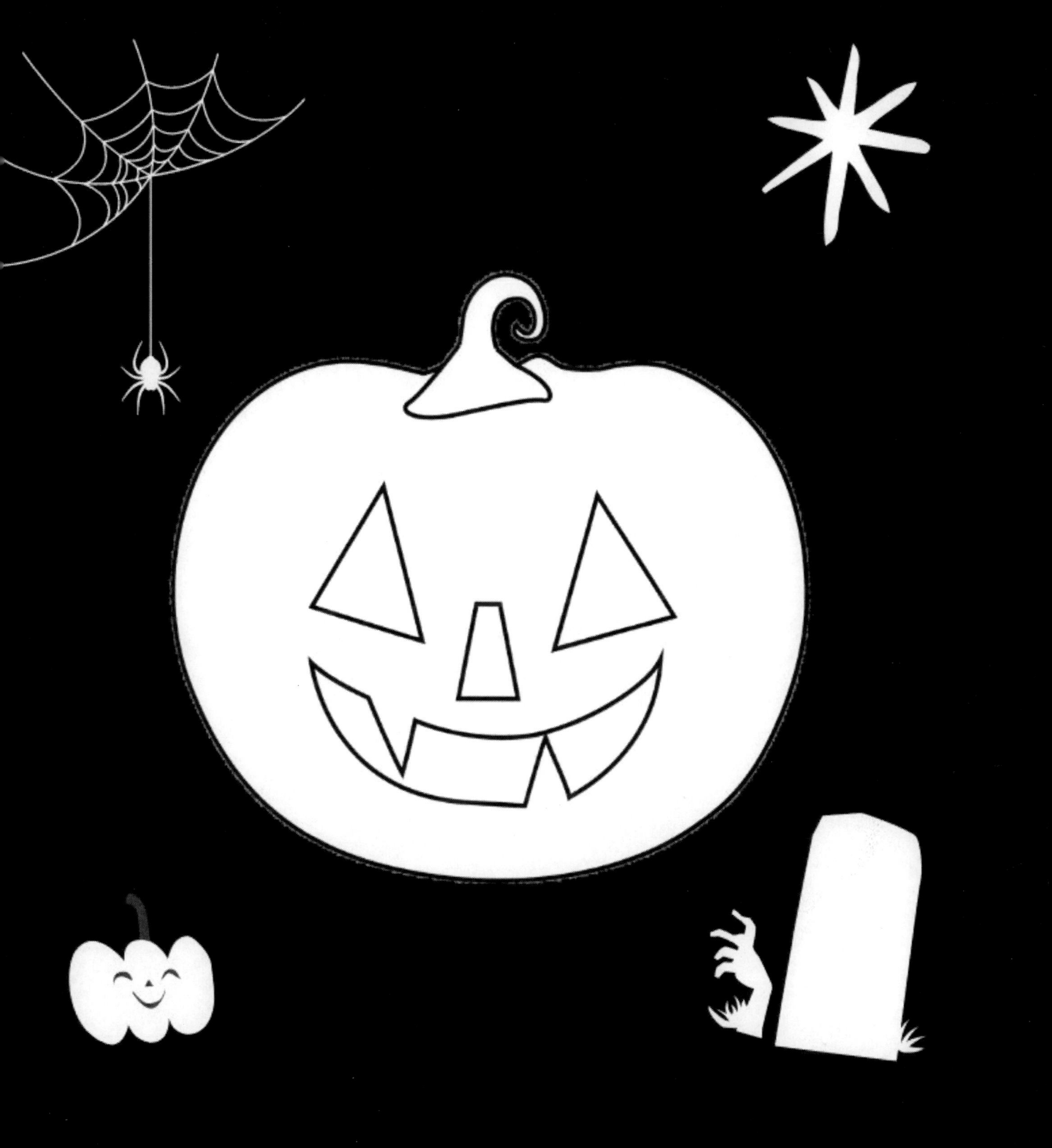

Thank you for purchasing our product.

it's really helpful for us, it means a lot.

Please leave a review for us.

Our Products

Made in United States
North Haven, CT
29 October 2022

26075314R00015